A Collection of Heartfelt Poems

Monica R. Harley

A publication of

Eber & Wein Publishing

Pennsylvania

A Collection of Heartfelt Poems

Copyright © 2013 by Monica R. Harley

All rights reserved under the International and Pan-American copyright conventions. No part of this book may be reproduced, stored in a retrieval system, or transmitted in any form, electronic, mechanical, or by other means, without written permission of the author.

Library of Congress
Cataloging in Publication Data

ISBN 978-1-60880-266-1

Proudly manufactured in the United States of America by

Eber & Wein Publishing
Pennsylvania

A Collection of Heartfelt Poems

A Collection of Heartfelt Poems

Inner Beauty

Inner beauty reflects the unique design of a person's well-being.
Inside every soul there is an attractiveness without seeing.
The depths of a person's beauty reveals who they really are.
In life, people can be seen as lovely and treated like a star.
This inner beauty is so special that it can make a person shine.
Every day a person can live life feeling good and choose to dine.
With beauty inside of people, one can perceive living in the world as good.
Also, living life can be easier if inner beauty is understood.

Monica R. Harley

Each Day Is a Gift from God

Each day is a gift from God
because He knows life's plan.
Throughout the day different things
happen unknown to man.
When the sun rises every morning
God controls the weather for the day.
Spiritual people appreciate each day
even when they have debts to pay.
Living life in a big world is complicated
but God is there in a high place.
He wants religious people to devote their life
to him with good grace.
God creates each day
with the intention of being adored.
His gift of life every day
will always make Him Lord.

The Qualities of My Soul Mate

My soul mate should be educated with a career.
He needs to love living life without fear.
I want him to love me completely with all of his soul.
Special times together should always make me feel whole.
His personality should be caring, loving, diligent, motivated, and smart.
These qualities would help me love him with all of my heart.
He should be spiritual and believe that life is a special gift from God.
By living this way, our relationship would be strong and not seem odd.
The possession of efficient qualities would create a great bond.
This special attraction would make me feel fond.

Monica R. Harley

My Lover's Mindset

My lover's mindset remains true;
his uncontrollable thinking helps me through.
These genuine ideas of him stay in my memory,
every day enhancing my sensory.
His warm thoughts of love arouse me mentally.
With his intellect I care for him gently.
My lover's mindset reminds me of my strength
to stay strong about his love to a certain length.
Days pass without him here;
all I want is to have him near.

A Collection of Heartfelt Poems

In My Dreams

In my dreams I imagine my lover,
how I want our love to go further.
I dream about him every hour of the day,
wishing he could come visit me and stay.
Images of him cloud my mind at night.
My constant deep thoughts tell me his love is right.
My everlasting visions are sensual,
with him our lovemaking is always consensual.

Monica R. Harley

My Spiritual Self

Every day spirits of people follow me.
I hear them so much that no one can see
how uncontrollable the sounds seem.
Without someone present my spirit is clean.
When I close my eyes these spirits are in my mind.
During the day they consume my thoughts until I find
the time at night to relax and dream of a perfect place
in hopes that I will live a happy life in the right space.

A Collection of Heartfelt Poems

My True Inspiration

I wake up every morning to the daylight outside.
Knowing that it is a brand new day makes me feel good inside.
Going outside to enjoy the sunshine gives my life meaning.
Sometimes I feel so refreshed that I can do a lot of cleaning.
On a pretty day, I am intrigued to go walking.
Lounging outside inspires me without people talking.
When the day ends, I look forward to tomorrow
without feeling any sorrow.
My true inspiration of the outdoors uplifts me every day,
so I can always do an outdoor activity the right way.

Monica R. Harley

The Sounds of Spirits

Spiritual sounds of people are within me.
The invisible presence of them won't let me be.
During my everyday living, I am not alone.
Spirits are present without a special tone.
The spiritual side of myself gives me joy
because the sounds of spirits do not annoy.
I am not afraid of sounds that are near.
I want to continue to live my life without fear.

A Collection of Heartfelt Poems

The Morning Ignites My Soul

In the morning my soul quickens to rise.
I do not refuse to wake or despise.
My soul energizes with glory to the morning light,
feeling high-spirited without a fight.
The frequent dreams of morning remain clear.
They ignite my soul with cheer.
Living life is essential in the early part of the day
to enjoy this happiness in a special way.
Looking forward to future mornings are my ultimate goal.
My morning awakening sparks the role of my soul.

Monica R. Harley

My Dream Life in the Summer

For my dream life in the summer,
I want to spend my time outdoors.
On the first day of summer
I will lounge under the palm trees until I want more.
Time to swim in a swimming pool
on a warm breezy day.
Staying active in the pool
keeps me alive so I can stay.
To continue my life in the summer,
I want to go to the beach to clear my head.
Being around water
makes me feel happy instead.
This dream life of the summer
always gives me something to look forward to.
The outdoors is where I feel
I have something to do.

In My Prayers

Every night I thank God for helping me survive another day.
I wake up the next morning with a new prayer to pray in a special way,
for God's unconditional love to guide me through life
without experiencing a lot of pain that cuts my soul like a knife.
My prayers to God are straight from my heart.
They give me a sense of purpose with a new start.
With God in my life I can achieve any goal,
because His everlasting love makes me whole.

Monica R. Harley

How I Love You

I love you like the purity of water in an ocean.
My heart always beats for you in a different motion.
As days go by without your love, life becomes unique.
To live every day my soul longs to love you with a different technique.
In the absence of your love, my heart grows fonder.
I love you so much that I do not need to ponder.
How I love you uplifts my soul in delight.
This feeling of love arouses me every night.

Life in the Winter

Life is complex for the average person in the winter.
In the morning, people have to scrape the frost off their vehicles carefully without getting a splinter.
On a cold snowy day with icy roads, businesses and schools close.
Adults and children have to stay home and wear layers of clothes.
A warmer winter day enables the sun to melt the snow off the roads.
With a snow truck, the snow is pushed to the grass in loads.
Living life in the winter can be fun if you like cold weather.
The best way to stay warm is to wear leather.
To complete the winter season, a person must eat a warm food.
This ensures that people stay in a wholesome mood.

Monica R. Harley

The Meaning of Friendship

A friend is someone to talk to.
This special person is there to help you through.
When bad times in life bring you down,
a friend can uplift your spirit so you do not frown.
In sadness, you are so hurt that you cry.
With a friend you are not alone because you have a special tie.
A caring friendship will grow over time.
Having a special someone makes you feel fine.
The love of a friend will stay true.
When you realize how the love and support grew.

The Strength of Friendship

When you are in need a friend will be there,
treating you with the highest care.
Throughout the journey of life you have someone to call.
This assures you that a friend will be present when you fall.
The strength of friendship is a priceless bond of love,
it can make you feel something from above.
Friendship is unbreakable when you share openly.
A friend can counsel you outspokenly.

Monica R. Harley

The Magnificent Outdoors

On any day of the year,
the outdoors can resemble peace on earth.
With the leaves on the trees changing to the season,
the climate has worth.
The outdoor temperature
gives life meaning.
This enables people
to maintain their lawns for cleaning.
In outdoor life, some people are motivated
to engage in an activity.
Living life outside on a nice warm day
encourages an athlete's productivity.
The magnificent outdoors
is a pleasant place to live on a nice day.
People can achieve happiness
even when the sky is gray.
Outdoor life is fulfilling
to people who love different types of weather.
Good living outside happens
when they are happy together.

A Collection of Heartfelt Poems

Wanting Your Love

Thinking of your love makes me want you by my side.
I was so hurt last night that I sat in bed and cried.
Your love is important to me because living alone is hard.
Sometimes I like to dream about you relaxing in the yard.
My desire is to be close to my lover once more.
In life, wanting your love does not make my heart feel torn.
Past memories of you are clear in my mind.
The world goes on every day and I feel left behind.
My longing to be close to you will stay the same,
knowing that your love for me was not a game.

Monica R. Harley

Friendship Can Last a Lifetime

Friendship can last a lifetime when there is trust.
It is a special bond that is honest and just.
The passing years enable a friendship to grow.
A lot of pleasant time together will show
how one can survive better with the other.
Life with a close friend is so great
that his or her feelings do not smother.
With a lifetime of friendship, a person can achieve any goal.
This is because he or she does not feel worthless
or left in a hole.
Friendship can last when both people share what's on their mind.
By doing this, each person can listen and be kind.

Life on a Rainy Day

To begin living life on a rainy day
a person needs to wear the right clothes,
because sometimes the temperature is unpredictable
and nobody knows.
People need to wear raincoats
and carry umbrellas to stay dry.
Business people with demanding careers
can be restricted to fly.
Staying indoors on a rainy day
is the best way to avoid the nasty weather.
If a person needs to go outdoors,
he or she can wear a hat and leather.
Life on a rainy day
can be relaxing in a house.
The end of the day can make people feel
important with their spouse.

Monica R. Harley

Can You Love Again

Can you love again?
How can you love again after all the pain
and heartache one has caused to you?
Oh, if I could take away the pain with
one sweet gentle kiss.
Would you be satisfied with that?
But how much satisfaction can one gain from a
kiss meaning to take away the pain?
My heart yearns for a love.
I had one before, one that was as sweet as yours,
For I have wronged you once before and maybe more,
but can you find it in your heart to forgive?
For without your forgiveness, I can't bear to live.
All I ask from you is can you love me again?
For that will be when my true happiness can begin.

My Lost Lover

Alone in my thoughts I think of the love I once knew,
the lover that I came near to.
This man's touch and embrace were the ones I became accustomed to,
whose gentle caresses and touches took my breath away and brought me tears of joy.
Being in his presence was something I deeply enjoyed.
The softness of my lips pressed against his brought me pure delight.
For then I knew our love was right.
His head ever so gently resting upon my breast brought my lover closer to my heart.
Feeling the connectedness of my love reassured me that we would never part.
Now that I have parted from him I feel as if part of me is missing.
At night, I miss our tender loving and kissing.
I think of him whenever my deepest desire fills my heart,
to be close to him even after we part.

Monica R. Harley

The Meaning of To Be Loved

To be loved is fulfilling,
a feeling that gives life meaning.
To be loved satisfies a person's well-being.
When needs are demanding, people require care,
even when a loved one is not there.
To be loved is an expression of emotion
without a special potion.
To be loved is the natural ability
to reciprocate another without agility.

My Heart Desires

My heart desires to be with my lover.
I cannot go any further
without expressing what he means to me.
Thinking of him fills my heart with glee.
Every day I live life with him on my mind,
I always tend to find.
Life's obstacles could not get in the way,
even when he lives away.
With him gone I wonder if he still treasures
my heart and what I desire to measure.
The depth of his heartfelt love will remain
in my memory to maintain.
What my heart desires will forever be the same.

Monica R. Harley

His Will to Love

This will to love is crystal clear,
so clean and powerful that it cheers
the soul of unique balance and stability.
With this love I gain the ability
to care with all my heart,
to ensure that we will never part.
In hopes that the world goes on with you and I,
I will always hold you in the center of my eye.
This will to love is one that most desire,
so much that it sparks a fire.
My heart yearns for this love every day
in a different special way.
With love we can overcome barriers
and develop a system of carriers
that will allow us to excel in life
without more envy and strife.
All in all his will to love is safe,
mostly in living in good faith.

Do You Love Still

Do you love still?
With warm sincerity and will,
the seasons pass real fast
without knowing if you had a blast.
You in my heart
assures that we will never part.
Still I wonder if I am still in your life
because without everyday living with you there is strife.
Days have gone by and you are always on my mind.
Anytime of the day while consuming my thoughts I still find
time for you to withdraw from the world
and embrace my soul in your enticing world.
This love will always be the fruit of good.
Do you love in a way to be understood?
Without your love I will not be able to live well,
to the point that you can tell
that my love for you will never die.
If hate in the world was only resolved with an eye for an eye.

Monica R. Harley

My Enticing Soul

My enticing soul sets on fire
when I think of the man I desire.
My racing thoughts about him are confusing
because he was never soul abusing.
With his natural loving soul I cherish life
to stand by his side without strife.
In my dreams my soul relaxes with joy,
knowing that this man was not a toy.

A Collection of Heartfelt Poems

Anger in My Life

During any time of the day I feel anger and displeasure.
Sometimes these feelings are too deep to measure.
This emotion can consume my thoughts on a bad day.
With anger in my life, it causes me to lose my way.
I get violent tendencies when I become confused.
They affect my life so much that I feel used.
Being angry is not the way I want to continue to live.
Instead I want to live free from fury and give.
Moving away from the South can uplift my soul.
In life, without anger I can accomplish any goal.

Monica R. Harley

Unwanted

I am not wanted by people who are supposed to be close to me.
Life in the South is really horrible because I am not free.
Every morning I wake up feeling isolated and alone.
This is because my feelings of loneliness appear unknown.
The hours of the day go by without a caring person near.
Living in the South unwanted hurts me every year.
I do not understand why distant people moved me here without a friend.
Without a close person in my life I cannot live to the end.
Being unwanted is how I will feel until I move away.
In the world, I try to live in good faith and pray.
During the holiday season I continue to feel unwanted and withdrawn.
All I can do to forget the pain is lounge outside on the lawn.

Sad and Alone

I am sad and alone because I have a mood disorder.
Throughout the day I am sane and can stay in order.
When I stay alone indoors my thoughts are bad.
They tend to control my mind and make me mad.
These feelings of being sad and alone break my heart most of the time.
This is what makes me want to go to the streets and commit a crime.
Without a close friend or relative I do not want to live in society.
The sadness and loneliness in a day does not cause me anxiety.
To finish a sad day alone I go to bed early at night.
In my dreams, I imagine a life that is fulfilling and right.

Monica R. Harley

Out of Place

I feel out of place every day
because I am away from my birth place.
Distant people changed my home several times
without showing their face.
In life, I walk around
with emptiness in my heart.
This out-of-place feeling
makes me slower to start.
Days go by at my current shelter
feeling incomplete.
I live life with the natural tendency
to walk in the street.
The morning sunlight keeps me awake
to face another day.
Knowing that God exists
encourages me to pray.
At the end of the day I think of a life
at a similar place of my home state,
hoping that I can begin to live
every day without hate.

Watching Television Is Lazy

Watching television is lazy
because it can make you fat.
A heavy television watcher is very unproductive
and he/she does not chat.
The more hours out of the day with a TV
are used in a negative way.
All people want to do
is drink alcohol, eat a lot, and lay.
Instead of productive working,
a lazy person just stares at TV.
Lazy people stay indoors so much
that TV stops them from being free.
At night, people tend to continue to watch TV
because they are greedy.
They are not very bright
and sometimes needy.
When television is needed for the news,
lazy people don't know how to act.
This daily habit of all day TV watching
is not just real, it is a fact.

Monica R. Harley

Life Without Love

Life without love is emptiness and pain.
It is living alone in fear with nothing to gain.
The feeling of loneliness runs deep through the veins.
Living this way keeps a person in bondage and chains.
Throughout the journey of life without love people are sad.
During the day they stay isolated and get mad.
When the day ends, a person is left without a caring friend.
No love in life makes it harder to live in the world until the end.
On a nice warm day, outdoor life without love is difficult to stand.
For a person to live fully, he/she needs to take a loving hand.

A Collection of Heartfelt Poems

On My Mind

During the day I think about you being with me,
wishing that we could relive our time together and be free.
My thoughts about you increase when I see my love tattoo.
This is a reminder of how my love poems get me through.
When time goes by I always remember how you made me feel.
Knowing that you loved me makes me miss a meal.
Before I go to bed at night, your loving technique is on my mind,
hoping that we could be close again and stay kind.

Monica R. Harley

Racing Thoughts

Racing thoughts are a negative side effect of my mood disorder.
They make me say and do things out of order.
Every time this happens I want to walk alone in the street.
I feel the need to wander outdoors without taking a seat.
Sometimes my thoughts race so fast that I forget what to say.
Living life with this symptom gets harder during the day.
When I stop thinking clearly I begin to lose focus on how to live.
This causes me to hate others and not give.
To slow my racing thoughts I write about my current mood.
It helps me clear my head so I don't get emotional and overeat food.

A Broken Heart

A broken heart happens when people really hurt you.
This is a bad feeling that makes you feel blue.
Knowing this pain causes you to withdraw and cry.
The people who were supposed to love you left you to die.
Not having a close relative every day hurts you more.
It is hard to fix a broken heart because you are tore.
In life, this painful heartache is difficult to bear.
To get help with a broken heart you can turn to God in prayer.

Monica R. Harley

Unemotional People

Unemotional people live without opening their hearts.
They are incomplete around others and slow to start.
Life is empty when people do not choose to feel.
This makes it hard to live in the world because these people are not real.
When a person does not show emotion he/she is not normal.
Every day is difficult to live without being formal.
During life's obstacles unemotional people are not there to care.
Most of them close their hearts and do not share.
In the morning, these people cannot awake with a touching soul.
At night, they stay withdrawn and are never whole.

An Unhappy Life

An unhappy life occurs when people feel out of place.
They do not belong in a certain state because they have a different face.
The feelings of loneliness and isolation make life hard.
Unhappy people who like the outdoors tend to lounge in the yard.
The unhappy life hurts people who want a friend to talk to.
This lifestyle is unpleasant and people cannot live true.
To make life better people need to move to a new place that will uplift their soul.
With a better life people are more likely to live with a purpose and role.

Monica R. Harley

Emotional Pain

Emotional pain hurts people who listen to their heart.
Living life is very difficult because pain is the worst part.
Threats from other people can damage a person inside.
Feelings of abuse cause him or her to lose pride.
Every day people suffer from a pain that runs deep.
This kind of torment impairs a person's nightly sleep.
In the world, people experience emotions that harden their soul.
The big world makes them feel left behind in a dark hole.

A Lonely Soul in a Big World

A lonely soul in a big world
is how I feel any time of the day.
In life, loneliness consumes my thoughts
so much that I stray.
With many people in the big world,
I do not have a significant other.
I always feel rejected
because I have a bad relationship with my mother.
Being lonely hurts my soul
without thinking about the pain.
Everyday living is not easy
with no one to talk to and be sane.
While the big world goes on,
I get the sense that people do not care.
These lonely feelings break my heart
even when I turn to God in prayer.
At the end of the day,
my lonely soul stays incomplete.
To live a better life,
I need to avoid walking alone in the street.

Monica R. Harley

Meeting My Significant Other

Meeting my significant other
is what I really want to do.
In my heart, I know there is someone special
in the world for me too.
During the day, I think of nice places
to meet my charming man.
Wanting to meet him encourages me
to search daily without a plan.
Living life every day
is hard without a comforting mate.
On the day we meet
it will be fate.
My heart's desire to be with my significant other
will not change.
This man will meet me with a good heart
without being strange.

Lost Without God

Sometimes I feel lost without God
because I get lonely during the day.
When I think of God's love
I focus on goals so I do not stray.
Life's obstacles make me lose my spiritual direction.
I feel like I have to live
without worshipping God in a particular section.
This feeling of no direction
causes me pain when I am alone.
The desires of my heart
are hidden deep, and are not known.
God is the one to love me completely
so I can live the right way.
His love satisfies my need of acceptance
so I do not get bored and lay.
Every day I feel lost
but God can show me what to do.
He can boost my spirit by hearing my prayers
and loving me too.

Monica R. Harley

A Painful Heartache

A painful heartache is what I feel when I think of you.
This emotional pain hurts deeply and makes me blue.
The heartache causes me to isolate and miss you by my side.
I constantly think of your love knowing that you never lied.
Your loving in the past was true with desire and skill.
With you next to me, I felt secure with a strong will.
My heartache continues without you in my heart.
To make this pain end, I need to know if your love was smart.

Empty Inside

Empty inside is how I feel
when I see the morning light.
My heart feels empty
without a special someone to make it right.
This feeling makes me want to meet
and marry a man for true love.
Living this way will fill my heart
so I can show the world what I am made of.
The emptiness brings pain
to my soul every day.
I dream of moving to a happy place
where I can live my own way.
A fulfilling life is what I need
to replace the pain inside.
Knowing my soul is empty
makes me want my future mate by my side.
At night, I shut out the world
and meditate on having a spouse.
Loving life will be easier with my significant other
with me at a house.

Monica R. Harley

Not My Home

In life, I feel like my current southern shelter is not my home.
Distant people chose to change my home as a child so I tend to roam.
Living is difficult knowing that I was born in a state affiliated with the northern states.
I do not remember moving to the South on certain dates.
As a child, I did not receive a lot of attention in a particular place.
What hurt me the most was that I was taken from my northern home space.
To be happy, I need to move to a place similar to where I came from.
The day I move to a special space will be the first time that I won't feel dumb.

An Endless Passion

An endless passion with my future spouse is what I dream of.
I want to meet and be with this man for love.
This yearning is what makes me focus on my daily goal,
to live life close to my significant other with all my soul.
The passion between us is unbreakable in my mind.
With him in my heart I know our love is blind.
Days continue to go by with me dreaming of who you are.
When I think of meeting you, I hope our instant attraction will go far.
My constant desire to marry a special man for love remains the same.
Every day I believe our endless passion will be a hot flame.

Monica R. Harley

Deep Desires

What can I say about a desire so deep that no one will understand?
To love another whom those close to you do not accept is difficult to stand.
I feel this desire to be with the one who sparks my fire but unforeseen circumstances
prevent me from satisfying my craving,
so much that my passions for him are raging
to the point where I only imagine the closeness of his body pressed against mine,
Remembering how our movements together made me feel fine.
His every touch and kiss brought me pure pleasure,
especially the night he entered my secret treasure.

www.ingramcontent.com/pod-product-compliance
Lightning Source LLC
Chambersburg PA
CBHW031659040426
42453CB00006B/352